Year Out

A Rough Guide to Gaining Professional Experience

Roger Harper

RIBA Publications

First Published as
A Student's Guide to the First Year in an Architect's Office
for the Education Department of the
Royal Institute of British Architects by RIBA Publications
First Edition 1989
Second Edition 1999
Year Out
© Roger Harper 2000

Published by RIBA Publications
Construction House, 56-64 Leonard Street, London, EC2A 4LT

ISBN 1 85946 056 9

Product Code: 21006

Publisher: **Mark Lane**
Consultant Editor: **Sarah Lupton**
Designed by: **Red Hot Media, Suffolk**
Printed by: **Dennis Barber Graphics & Print, Suffolk**

Acknowledgements

First edition, 1989

I should like to thank the following for their very generous help and advice:

John Bennetts, Thames Polytechnic and RIBA Co-ordinator for Professional Training;

Martin Bridge, Office Manager, Building Design Partnership, Manchester;

Barbara-Ann Campbell, author of the booklet *How to plan your Year-out* published by the Bartlett School of Architecture, University of London;

Ronald Green, architect and senior partner, Casson Conder Partnership, London;

Michael Taylor, Assistant Chief Architect, Property Services Department, Royal County of Berkshire;

Brenda Vale, Department of Architecture, University of Sheffield;

Alan Willis, Essex County Architect and Chairman of the RIBA Professional Studies and Training Sub-Committee.

In particular, I owe a special debt of thanks to David Chappell for his detailed advice and encouragement. If the student requires a more comprehensive and advanced treatment of the matters briefly discussed in this book he or she is strongly advised to refer to the excellent publications by David Chappell.

Advice has also come from many of the Practical Training Advisers for the various Schools of Architecture, including:

Graham Brown, Portsmouth Polytechnic;

Stanley Cox, formerly of University of Wales;

Kenneth Herbert, University of Sheffield;

Kenneth Holdstock, Plymouth Polytechnic;

Roderick Males, University of Manchester;

David Nicholson-Cole, University of Nottingham;

Roger Tillotson, University of Newcastle upon Tyne.

Financial support was made available in the form of a Research Award from the Architects Registration Council of the United Kingdom.

Finally, my thanks to the many students of the University of Sheffield Department of Architecture who replied to the original survey questionnaires. It is hoped that their experiences and advice, which form the basis of this guide, will be of benefit to all students everywhere.

Second edition, 1997

I am indebted to my colleague Simon Pilling, until recently Practical Training Adviser, School of Architectural Studies, University of Sheffield, for his advice on the revision and up-dating of the present text.

Year Out, 2000

RIBA Publications would like to thank John Bennetts, Stanley Cox and Sarah Lupton for the relevant revision and up-dating of the present text.

Dr Roger H. Harper
Reader in Architecture
School of Architecture
University of Sheffield
Sheffield S10 2TN

Contents

Why Practical Training?
An Introduction

This guide is intended to help students of architecture who are about to embark on their first year's practical training and have decided to work in an architect's office.

For most students this time in practice is the first major break from a way of life conditioned by many years in school and college. From now on a student is assumed to have some basic skills, to understand how to take responsibility and to earn a position of trust, and he or she will be paid on the assumption that the job will be done properly.

The **Year Out** must not be undertaken lightly, yet at the same time it should be enjoyable. New and exciting ideas may be explored, and new friends and contacts made. It will generate confidence and maturity, as well as providing an opportunity to plan for the future. Some students may find no problem in all this but, having spent some time questioning students and their supervisors in offices, it is clear that this is a critical period and one that can be, occasionally, quite traumatic. Some form of guidance, however elementary, may therefore be helpful and reassuring. Areas of doubt and feelings of isolation can be overcome. Almost everything is covered in this guide, from the first thoughts about choosing the type of office through to the problems that may occur in the first weeks in the new job.

Remember that nearly all the qualified architects who will be working with students will have gone through a similar stage themselves, but remember also that it may have been some time ago and their memories of what it was like will have faded. Being busily occupied day by day, they have established a rhythm and way of working that they now take for granted. They will need a little time to adjust to the new student just as much as he or she will need time to adjust to them.

The RIBA Professional Experience and Development Scheme requires a minimum of two years' practical training before a student can take the Examination in Professional Practice, frequently referred to as Part Three. A minimum of one year must be spent in an architect's office in the United Kingdom. As an alternative to working in an architect's office in the first year of practical training, a student may choose to work in the associated professions, with members of the building team or in research and development, but in that case the second year MUST be spent in an architect's office in the United Kingdom.

This guide is by way of an unofficial supplement to the RIBA Professional

Experience and Development Record that gives the rules and objectives of practical training, and it is absolutely essential for every student to get a copy well before starting work in an office and to read the introductory pages very carefully.

The student should also identify his or her 'Practical Training Adviser' – the member of staff in the school who is in charge of this topic, and who will liaise with the student during the year in the office. There is no harm in the student talking at any stage in the school course to the 'Practical Training Adviser' about planning the year in the office.

The person who is in overall charge of the student whilst he or she is in the office is called the 'Office Supervisor' but in this guide the informal term 'boss' is used to refer to the person for whom the student will be directly working. So the 'boss' may be a partner, associate, group or team leader, job architect or whatever, although in some cases the 'boss' will be the 'Office Supervisor' as well. The 'Office Supervisor' must be an experienced qualified architect.

While every effort has been made to ensure that the factual information in this guide is as accurate as possible, neither the author, the RIBA nor the publishers can accept responsibility for any mistakes or omissions. They would nevertheless welcome any corrections or additions for future editions.

1

Where Will You Work?

The Various Types of Offices

The fundamental difference between offices concerns how they were established and financed. A *private office* is an independent concern, ranging in size from a one-man band to a large enterprise, such as Building Design Partnership. It keeps itself alive by the income received from fees from clients in respect of projects undertaken, and from these fees it pays its staff and overheads (office rents, heating, etc.). It stays in business to fulfil its contractual obligations to its clients and needs to earn a predetermined profit. Responsibility is towards the office as a whole and directly to the client who has placed the commission.

The other category is where *the architect's department is within a larger organisation* and is directly responsible in the first instance to the organisation itself and not to any outside client (although it still has to maintain its own viability and conform, of course, to professional standards, legislation, etc.), and is financed by the larger organisation. It is in a sense therefore more secure, but only so long as the larger organisation remains in business. Offices of this type fall into various categories:

(a) Architect's departments in, for example, public limited companies such as the larger scale retailers,

the larger building contractors such as Wimpeys or Laings, and major banks.

(b) Architect's departments within local authorities – the 'Town Hall' – dealing with predominantly housing, rehabilitation, schools, social welfare buildings, civic schemes of one sort or another and on a variety of levels.

(c) Departments within national or central government bodies – such as the Department for Education and Employment, Development Corporations or National Park Boards.

(d) Housing Associations.

Within this broad description there will obviously be a wide range of experience to be gained, and, from your point of view, there will be good and less good offices within each category. Clearly it is impossible to be more specific here, but it is important for you to understand where the different offices place their priorities since it colours their whole approach to their work and, in turn, affects how they see your role in their organisation.

From your point of view the size of the office is important. In a *small one-man band* you may get excellent experience, being close to all aspects of the job, seeing it from start to finish, dealing with everyone including the client and outside consultants as well as the contractor. There will be considerable pressure, it can be exciting, and it calls for initiative and self-confidence. The disadvantages are the possible personality problems of working with one or two other people for any length of time, and the 'all or nothing' state of tension which can exist. There is sometimes no 'fall-back' position, and the office can seem precarious. There is also the danger that you may be left in the office to answer the phone (it may be the next client at the other end of the phone) while the boss is on site or in other client meetings.

The *medium-size office* has fewer risks. It may be subdivided into smaller groups or teams which operate rather like small independent offices, but with the back-up of the rest of the office. It usually has a good range of jobs, at different stages.

The *large office* can be very stimulating, with large jobs, plenty of variety, plenty of people to meet and groups to move through. It is likely to have facilities such as a good library information service, frequent office discussions – about projects and architecture in general – and 'in-house' consultants who can sort things out quickly and from whom you can learn a lot. Disadvantages are that you might get 'lost' by being put on a very large job doing something rather lengthy and tedious and without the opportunity to get a variety of experience within the office as required for the period of practical training.

Lines of Command and Responsibility

Span and line of control are critical in all offices. It is not always easy to see at the outset how this works, even if the office is aware of the concept, but at interview stage it should be possible to ask how the lines of command and responsibility work. They may be either clear and consistent, or muddled and ambiguous. The claim that, 'Oh, we usually sort something out' is often a sign that things are not too business-like. If this is the case, you may find problems in carrying out work for different people, often simultaneously, or having one person's request override another.

Your Basic Employment Rights

Your employer has a duty to pay you, provide work for you, indemnify you (i.e. secure you against legal responsibility), reimburse you if you incur reasonable expenses in doing your work and look after your safety.

You, in turn, cannot, without agreement, delegate your duties to anyone else. You must obey the lawful instructions given to you by your employer, take reasonable care when on your employer's business and generally 'demonstrate good faith' such as taking care of confidential information.

When appointed you should receive a written statement outlining the following: the names of the parties involved (the employer and yourself); the date of starting work; the date of finishing; the title of the job (architectural assistant or similar); the period of notice should either side wish to terminate the job; the rate of pay and when you will be paid (weekly, monthly, etc.); hours of work; amount of holiday allowed and any sick pay provision. In your Year Out you will not qualify for maternity rights (i.e. six months maternity pay, time for ante-natal care and the right to return after the birth), since you will not have worked the necessary two years in continuous employment up to the eleventh week before the expected birth. Absence on compassionate grounds (e.g. to attend a family funeral), is entirely at your employer's discretion and you have no right to it, nor to unpaid leave.

You should be aware of legislation designed to protect employees, including the Race Relations Act 1976, the Sex Discrimination Act 1975, the Disabled Persons (Employment) Act of 1944 as amended by the 1958 Act and the recent Disability Discrimination Act 1995.

Students who are nationals and full passport holders of the other 14 member states of the European Union or from the countries which, though not part of the EU are within the European Economic Area (Norway, Iceland, Liechtenstein), have essentially the same employment rights in this country as UK nationals.

Students from outside the European Union or EEA will, unless exempt for some reason, only be able to take up work after the employer has obtained the requisite Training Work Permit. (Exemptions include Commonwealth citizens with a parent or grandparent born in the UK, and a few other special categories of people.) The employer will have to obtain a Training & Work Experience Scheme (TWES) work permit from the Overseas Labour Service of the Department for Education and Employment.

Most international students in the UK will have a stamp in their passport stating that they may take up employment with the permission of the Secretary of State for Education and Employment (i.e. once a work permit has been issued to the employer). Some students, however, will have a 'prohibition' stamp on their passport. If this is the case, a work permit could not be obtained unless successful representation was first made to the Home Office to have this stamp changed to a 'restriction'.

Termination of Employment
If termination of employment is not set down in the written terms of the appointment the period of notice on the employer's side is one week, if you have been continuously employed for over one month but less than two years. In your case, you need only give officially one week's notice if you have been employed for more than four weeks. You can take payment *in lieu* if you wish. Dismissal without notice can be given if you break your contract through misconduct, such as stealing, fighting, disobedience or total incompetence.

Redundancy
Should redundancy occur during your year in the office, you are not entitled to

any redundancy payment since you will not have completed the statutory two years of continuous employment. If you are made redundant through no fault of your own, your period of employment should still be considered to be valid for practical training requirements.

Insurance

It is worth checking the insurance position with your employer at the outset. Your employer is normally responsible for what you do when you are in his or her employment (this is called 'vicarious liability'), but if you, the employee, have been negligent, the 'injured party' could, if he or she wished, bring an action in tort directly against you. It is important, therefore, that the insurance policy is worded so as to give indemnity for you in respect of any such liability you might incur when working for the office. Being 'temporary', students may only have Third Party insurance cover, for example.

Health and Safety

The Health and Safety at Work Act 1974 covers all employees apart from the clergy and domestic servants. Under Section 2 of the Act, an employer must take reasonable steps to ensure the safety of those working for him or her. Under Section 3, no employer shall, in his or her work, endanger any other person not employed by him or her – so everyone is involved in this 'duty of care' to every other person.

Ask to see the office's written statement on health and safety on site. Take reasonable care of your own health and safety – particularly when on building sites and when surveying old buildings.

The rule when on site is always to wear sensible clothing and a 'hard hat'. Watch out for scaffolding and ladders (which should be tied securely); floorboards and stairs (which may be rotten underneath); loose equipment, holes and other unprotected areas. Not so obvious, but worth remembering, is to check that gas and electricity services have been disconnected. The possible lack of oxygen, if you have to go into confined spaces such as sewers or cellars, is another hazard; and there could be vermin, rats, wood decay by beetle plus hazards caused by vandals and children who may have entered the site illegally.

Drawings should always have the signature of your boss on them before they are issued. This not only shows that the drawing has been approved, but also that your boss or the office has taken the responsibility for them. Under the Health and Safety at Work Act 1974, it is the designer of something who is held responsible.

Appropriate Levels of Expectation and Responsibility

The RIBA *Architects' Handbook of Practice Management* sets out a system for grading jobs or people in an office. Only the first two grades are relevant here, and they are:

Grade A: A junior employee, often a student, performing simple jobs under strict supervision;

Grade B: An architect capable of handling, under supervision, small jobs, or working as part of a team on a large project.

You could expect to start at Grade A and, as you become established and more confident, find that your work begins to overlap with that of Grade B. Previous editions of the RIBA *Handbook of Architectural Practice and Management* described these two grades (then referred to as levels) in terms of the type of work involved, the level of initiative, the influence on others in the office and the responsibility involved. These are:

(a) Type of work which can be handled: At level A, you should be able to perform simple jobs offering little or no alternative methods and undertake simple analysis of problems for which logical answers are readily obtainable. At level B, you should be able to perform work offering a limited number of alternative methods and solve problems for which logical answers are not readily apparent and which have some effect on the other aspects of the job.

(b) Knowledge and initiative: At level A, no initiative is required; at level B, limited initiative is required – e.g. limited research into technical literature and knowledge of the more common types of materials.

(c) Influence on others: At level A, you should be able to execute simple instructions and have a minimum influence on the work of others. At level B, you should be able to

understand and execute clear instructions and be able to give simple, clear instructions.

(d) Responsibility: At level A you should be responsible for making minor decisions, with all your work being closely supervised. At level B, you should be responsible for making decisions affecting your own work, which must be reported to your boss. Parts of your work will be closely supervised.

Finding Out About the Offices: where to look for information

- Whose work do you admire? To work for a famous name is an attractive idea, but at this stage in your career it might be more valuable to consider somewhere with a sound reputation and a wide variety of good experience on offer. Find out what they have built, where their office is and how large it is. Look through *The Architects' Journal, Architectural Review, Building Design,* also the *RIBA Journal,* all of which have published 'Practice Profiles' and report on new buildings.

- The RIBA *Directory of Practices* and the RIAS *Directory of Scottish Chartered Architects' Offices* are the best sources to find out the size of private offices, the type of work which they undertake, the names of their major projects (try and visit one or two if you are really keen), the names of the partners and the addresses of the offices. The *Directory of Official Architects* gives information about local authorities, government agencies, etc. There is also the Association of Consultant Architects' *Illustrated Directory of Architects.*

- The RIBA Appointments Bureau has up to date information on a large number of practices, but is also extremely busy and is only rarely able to offer Year Out vacancies.

- *RIBANet,* the RIBA electronic conferencing service, carries Appointments Bureau information and has a Student Jobs Section (under the 'Study of Architecture' icon) to take over from the previous RIBA Practical Training Vacancies Bureau by providing employers and students with an immediate and flexible meeting point to advertise training vacancies and student skills.

- Ask the students in the years ahead of you where they went and what they recommend. They will also give you a good idea of the salary ranges on offer. Some offices like to retain links with certain schools. Not many offices advertise in the commercial journals for students for one year, but they do write to the schools and their advertisements should be on display. Even before applying you could ask to visit a practice, to see how they operate and to talk to students already working there. It may be somewhat one-sided, but you should get a 'feel' of how an office generally responds to students, whether they are welcoming, casual or dismissive.

- Keep an eye on the job-market overall to see which offices are advertising for fully qualified staff. Do they have a rapid turnover, which might be a cause for concern, or do they appear to be expanding, in which case they may well need student assistance?

Remember it is your choice in the end – not your school's – but check with your Practical Training Adviser. (Your school may require you to register formally for practical training and might operate a preferred office policy.) If it doesn't work out as you expected (and rarely are one's expectations ever completely fulfilled) don't do anything hasty, but do consult your Practical Training Adviser. There will be time to adjust when you come to your second period of practical training.

Working Abroad

To count under the RIBA Professional Experience and Development Scheme only a maximum of ONE year may be spent overseas. Note that working in the Republic of Ireland is currently regarded as overseas experience for the purposes of the RIBA Professional Experience and Development Scheme.

In recent years working abroad, either in Europe or in non-European countries, has assumed greater significance and continues to do so. It can be attractive and valuable work experience for many students, but it is worth noting these comments from students who have worked abroad:

'Working abroad will mean that you have to 'travel light', and may have to spend quite a bit of money unexpectedly at first', and
'Working abroad in a non-English speaking office can be lonely since you may not be able to follow the fast colloquial chat in the office, or the jokes.'

It is important to find out the relative cost of living. Salaries may appear high in relation to those here, but they must be seen in terms of accommodation rental charges, cost of food, travel, etc. You will also have to include the cost of air or sea travel, and accept that you will be somewhat 'isolated' from your contacts at home.

A good grasp of the language of the country you will be working in is obviously an advantage, and it pays to keep your language skills alive.

Freedom of movement to work in European Community countries without the need for a visa provides an opportunity to enrich your knowledge of the culture of other European countries and to make friends with people from different cultural and educational backgrounds.

Experience of living and working in other parts of the continent will broaden your awareness of the influences on design of climate, terrain and local tradition and of cultural influences from outside the present European Community. Free competitive movement of labour maximises the personal and economic potential of everyone, and a peaceful and creative future for Europe will be encouraged by the exchange of ideas in the architectural community.

The following extracts are from *A Student's Guide to Europe* by Caroline Jackson:

'The European Community Treaty provides for an end to discrimination based on nationality between workers – as regards employment, remuneration and other conditions of employment' (Article 48).

Apart from some very limited exceptions, this opens up the Community labour market to all citizens of the Member States, and governments cannot use high unemployment as an excuse to prevent such movement. Potential employees do not have to seek prior approval from the host country before starting work. You will not need a work permit; but in certain countries you will need a residence permit – the European Community still has very high unemployment, and over half the community jobless are under the age of 25, but you should not find it an insurmountable problem to find a short- to medium-term job.

There is a European system for exchanging information on job vacancies. SEDOC (French initials) supply addresses of employment services in specific towns or regions as follows:

- Agence Nationale pour l'Emploi, Service SEDOC 53 Rue General Leclerc F-92136 Issy-les-Moulineaux, France.

- Zentralsteue fur Arbeitsvermittlung SEDOC Ausgleichstelle Feuerbachstrasse 4246 D-6000 Frankfurt Am Main, Germany.

- Umotem, Servizio SEDOC Via Pastrengo 16 Roma, Italy.

- Directoraat generaal voor de Ardbeidsvoorziening Afdeling SEDOC Volmerlaan 1 Rijsijk Zh, Netherlands.

Guides to working in Europe are published by the RIBA and available from RIBA Publications. They are researched and written by Melanie Richardson, formerly at the University of Sheffield (now at De Montfort University), with support from an ARCUK Research Grant.

Designed to help UK students with Part 1 qualifications explore the possibility of gaining work experience in other EU countries, the guides cover living, seeking work, architectural practice and office routine. Each guide is prefaced with general information and includes a list of schools of architecture and a bibliography. Procedures included apply only to students who are citizens of, or have obtained resident status in, an EU member state.

Students should also be aware of the European Community programmes:

SOCRATES, a European funding programme for the development of education in Europe. This has, as one of its strands, the ERASMUS programme which aims to promote community-wide exchanges of students for study abroad, with financial support, and ultimately for transfer between courses across Europe.

LEONARDO DA VINCI, an EU vocational training programme, divided into three strands:

Strand I: Improving vocational training systems in the member states.
Strand II: Improving vocational training for undertakings and workers.
Strand III: Developing language skills, knowledge and the dissemination of information.

The focus is on initial and continuing vocational training through transnational pilot projects, exchanges, placements, etc.

Ask your school of architecture or your University's overseas office or careers advisory office for further details.

② Getting a job

What type of work are you looking for? Will it give you the sort of experience you need? Do you know what you need? For example, do you wish to follow a developing interest in, say, housing, or do you want a more general range of work? Do you need a type of work that will redress weaknesses in design or technology? Do you want to try a type of work that will be quite the opposite to that which you hope to do after final qualification? You may have been thinking about this during your earlier years and may have spent a few weeks in an office in the summer vacation, and so already have some idea of what type of office to go for – or to avoid – and useful contacts you may already have established.

Other personal factors may be relevant here, such as:

(a) Do you want to get away from the town where you have been a student for three years?

(b) Do you want to work in your hometown? It may be cheaper living at home, but there may be restrictions on your freedom;

(c) Consider the cost of living in larger cities, particularly London, with the difficulty of accommodation, the cost of transport and the time it might consume in commuting. Balance that against higher pay and the attractions of the bright lights, including the architectural highlights and the opportunity to hear and visit up-to-the-minute talks, exhibitions, etc.;

(d) Do you have hobbies – sailing, climbing etc. – which make particular locations attractive?

(e) Do you want to travel and work abroad?

The first step to getting a job is preparing an up to date curriculum vitae.

Your Curriculum Vitae
This is an outline of your education, qualifications, experience and interests, which you submit together with your letter of application for a job. It is an important document because it is the first thing the employer sees of you, and should be brief, effective and relevant. It has to catch the employer's eye and, while a personalised heading or simple 'logo' can be effective, it is better not to try any 'clever' gimmicks. Think about adding some (one or two only) A4 reductions of your drawings, but they should not detract at all from the text.

It should be type-written, black on white, well spaced, and at this stage in your career it will probably cover about two sides of A4.

It should give the following information, in this order:

- full name;
- date of birth;
- sex;
- nationality;
- personal information, e.g. married or single;

- your present permanent address, and your address in term-time, in full, with post code and a telephone number where you can be contacted easily;

- if you hold a current driving licence and if you own a car (but if you use it for business then beware – the insurance premiums may have to rise sharply);

- a photograph of yourself may be included;

- educational background. Previous education from secondary school stage (not primary school) through to your college career, listing all your achievements, prizes and awards;

- educational qualifications. List in chronological order all 'O' levels or 'GCSE' levels and 'A' or 'AS' levels (with grades) or, if your secondary education has been in Scotland, your 'O' Grades, Higher Grades or 'SYS' Grades, your Ordinary or Higher National Certificates or Diplomas, and your school of architecture examinations and degree classification;

- if you have had any sort of previous office experience (not necessarily architectural) then include that here also, with the name of the office and the dates when you worked there;

- any special skills such as working with computers, a good working knowledge of a foreign language, typing, model making, photography, and any other form of work experience;

- anything which has a bearing, even indirectly, on your ability to handle the job you are applying for, such as Duke of Edinburgh awards, writing articles on architectural matters, editing a college magazine, running a school or college society, designing theatre scenery, overseas travel and community work. Keep everything in chronological order so an employer can see how your career has progressed to date;

- references – list the full names, titles and addresses of two or three people who have known you for some time and who will be prepared to write on your behalf, if requested by the prospective employer, to vouch for your ability and character. Check that they are willing to do this for you before you apply for the job. Referees are often members of the staff in your school of architecture; others could be from another part of your life (but not relatives) who have responsible positions in society – a vicar, doctor, or headmaster.

Design the layout of your CV with care – it shows your future employer that you can 'design' and that you take care over such important matters.

The Letter of Application

When to start applying for jobs? There is no hard and fast rule but your Practical Training Adviser should be able to suggest the best times. If, however, you know where you want to go and think that an early application will secure the job, then go for it as soon as you like. It will be one less thing to think about as your examinations approach.

The New Year, from say February or March onwards, is generally a good time to apply. Much depends on the state of the market and demand, but by Easter the activity is usually in full swing. Some offices may retain your letter until they are in a position to know exactly what their staffing needs actually are. Others consider they can pick and choose and will wait until after the final exams. Some offices may wait to take students from certain schools only.

The building industry is subject to ups and downs and the job situation can rapidly change. When jobs are scarce some students have written thirty or forty letters without success, yet on other occasions when there is a boom, architects have been known to come from their office directly into the schools to persuade students to work for them.

It is usual to write, either 'out of the blue' to someone you want to work for, or in reply to an advertisement you have seen, or on a recommendation you have received. Telephoning or knocking on the door of the office itself is not usually recommended.

There is an art in letter writing. Use A4 paper. To write by hand or to type your letter is debatable. If your own handwriting is neat and clear it may add to the quality of your application and it may make it stand out among a number of more conventional typewritten letters. It can also show an employer that you can 'letter' clearly. But if in doubt, type the letter, but make sure that your signature is legible!

With the use of computers it is relatively easy to plan your letter, organise it on the sheet of paper and choose a suitable typeface. Don't overdo it and make an elaborate fancy design using every style of typeface under the sun! Remember always that you are showing that you are a good designer, in everything you do, and that includes designing your letter.

Put your address and phone number towards the top (usually right hand side) and the date below it. Then slightly lower down, on the left side, the full name and address of the person to whom you are writing.

About a third of the way down the page, begin with either 'Dear Sir' or 'Dear Madam' (which always concludes with 'Yours faithfully') or 'Dear Mr (Mrs or Ms) …' (which always ends with 'Yours sincerely'). You can usually discover the name of the person to whom you should be writing by telephoning the office. This can be a good idea since it not only ensures that your letter gets to the right person, but also shows a certain initiative. Head the letter with the title of the job for which you are applying and any reference number, and underline it. It is unwise to stray from this pattern.

Compose your letter to catch and hold the attention of the reader. Remember most practices will receive many regular applications. Yours must be focused and enthusiastic if it is going to rise above the others. Try and avoid opening with the words, 'I am a student at, etc.'. Nevertheless, you will have to mention somewhere near the beginning that you are at present a student in your third year (or equivalent) at a particular school of architecture.

Say that you wish to apply for the job, and that you are enclosing a curriculum vitae (and any other supporting documentation such as photographs or reduced copies of drawings). The value of sending photo-reduced copies of your work at this stage is, however, debatable because they are hard to see, you are not there to explain them, they add bulk and are expensive. They are best used for overseas applications only.

Say why you would like to work for that particular office. You may have some special reason, but don't eulogise unnecessarily. Be tactful in how you do this. Highlight any particular skills (which may also be on your CV) which you think they should respond to and which will be to your advantage.

Say when you could start work and when you would NOT be available for interview, for example immediately before and during your examinations. Don't mention anything about salaries at this stage.

Presentation is important. Space the letter out carefully on the page, so that it occupies the whole of one side evenly. Watch your spelling and don't rely on the spell-check in a word-processor. Send a stamped addressed envelope if you wish, it shows consideration and enthusiasm, but some offices may not reply even then!

If you have a physical disability it is wise to record that fact in your letter of application, but only if it is likely to affect your work directly, such as a difficulty with hearing or using stairs.

The office may respond immediately, but every office should at least acknowledge the receipt of your letter. They should in that case also say when they will get in touch again. They may wish to wait until a particular time before selecting a number of students for interview. You will have to decide whether you wish to wait for them. If you don't and you take another job elsewhere, then you must write and let that former office know.

The Interview:
Preparing and Presenting your Portfolio
- You will be expected to take along examples of your work. Take the work which you feel gives the best reflection of your range of experience and your capabilities – a variety, but not a rag-bag

collection. The variety will show the different types of projects and the different aspects of your work in terms of sketches, preliminary design, constructional studies, building science studies, final design drawings and photographs of models. You do not need to take every drawing, but have a sufficient number to show that you have tackled these various aspects. The interviewer is also interested to see how well you can draw and 'letter', as well as your design and technological knowledge.

- Rehearse how you will talk the interviewer through your work. Start with your best, which will probably be your degree work. Keep your drawings in order, on the same size paper (even if that means mounting small sketches, which will then look better than small scraps floating loose in your portfolio). It is useful if you have standardised your drawings to some extent, the same paper size and a title block for example, since this gives an impression of order, control and forethought.

- Keep the drawings flat in a portfolio. Never take them rolled up (they will be impossible to keep flat on a table during the interview) and consider reduction if you can afford it since A1 size portfolios are very cumbersome.

- Check the portfolio over with your tutor before you go and correct any mistakes there may be on the

drawings or be prepared to say how you would correct them if asked. Indicate that it is all your own work, or make it very clear, if you have been working as part of a group, which is your own work. All this is your responsibility and you must feel confident about every item you show, so leave out anything you can't justify or explain.

- It is worth including A4 size reports and essays because they further help to show the range of work you have covered. Many employers are often interested in your writing skills.

- Put a really attractive drawing on the top so that it is the first thing seen when the portfolio is opened on the desk. Have available a *brief* note about your projects, perhaps fixed to the corner of each. This might be the original programme issued by the school.

Try to keep the interest going by moving through your portfolio. Talk your way through, using the drawings to pace your account. Don't talk too much about each project as though you were justifying it to a tutor in college. A brief introduction to each project is best and the interviewer will then follow with any questions.

Find out something about the office beforehand, so that you will be able to talk intelligently about its work, naming a project or two that you admire or have visited.

Don't go to an interview 'just for practice'. It may sound a bright idea, but it will show if you are not serious, and harm will be done, not only to you but to any other students who may follow. However, do beware of jobs that don't really exist. A vague indication that there might be a job vacancy in a month or two is not acceptable. It is risky and either may not come to anything or may change, in the event, to a different type of job altogether. Remember, if you accept a job from one office, while you still have another interview pending at another office, let the second office know and cancel the interview appointment.

Before you set off make sure you know exactly where you are going. Look at the timetables in advance, consult a map of the town you are going to and photocopy or sketch the relevant area you will be making for. Carrying a large and heavy portfolio through a large town on a hot day is no joke, so this might be the one day to afford a taxi! It is rare for the office to pay your travelling expenses. Take the letter requesting you to attend with you, and get there a little early so that you can unwind and take stock of your surroundings. If you are delayed, telephone immediately to let the office know there is a problem and when you expect to arrive – they will understand.

Self-presentation: Some General Advice
- Dress naturally and comfortably – but not scruffily. Your appearance does matter and 'first impressions' really do count – if you take the job, you will be 'on show' and part of the office 'image'.

- Actually say 'Good-morning', look the person who is talking to you straight in the eye, and try and remember at least the name of the principal person who is interviewing you. It looks good if you can refer to him or her by name later in the interview, or if you have to phone up later with a question.

- Jot down a few notes beforehand of things you may want to ask in the interview. Take a pencil and scale with you – it looks efficient! Try and be as natural as possible without straining and without being pretentious or pompous.

- Listen carefully to the question(s) asked.

- Don't talk in a way which you think the interviewer wants to hear, just be yourself. There may be an awkward question. It is rare for this to be done deliberately in order to trip you up or to embarrass you, but if it happens, and you don't have the answer immediately, keep calm, and say you don't know – but say how you would go about finding the answer.

- A good interviewer will understand you are a little nervous and try to ease the situation, even by just talking about your journey or the weather.

Try to identify the person you may be working under, and keep a sharp look out around the office. If they don't show you round, actually ask to have a look, preferably in your own time, so that you can talk to other students there. See what people are wearing and sense if the atmosphere is relaxed or formal.

If the interview seems to be going well you could ask about the following more detailed matters:

(a) Ask them how they see their responsibility towards students in terms of their educational advancement. Your school may require you to attend seminars or courses in connection with your practical training, and this obligation should be explained and cleared with the office before accepting any job.

(b) Ask about overtime. Do they do it and do they encourage it? If so, do they pay for it? It is generally expected that you will have to do overtime at some stage or other, not continuously, but whenever there is a particular deadline to meet.

(c) Ask about holiday arrangements.

(d) If you intend doing any private work in your own time, check the office has no objection. It will always be at your own risk and it is not the office's responsibility in any way, but may interfere with their dealings with their own clients.

Salary

Discussion of possible salary is tricky. You should have some idea beforehand of what people in your position in that type of office are getting paid. Check the salaries offered with those shown in similar current job advertisements in your school. Alternatively, your PTA may be able to advise you as the school may have a record of salaries. You may feel you could take a lower salary if your living expenses are likely to be low and you like the look of the office, but on the other hand, if what they offer you seems on the low side ask to be allowed to consider it further. If they offer you a job, you don't have to accept there and then. They should write to you and confirm all the arrangements, including salary (as discussed earlier).

Religion

If you have a religious belief which makes strict demands in terms of eating, fasting, washing, prayer or other ritual observances, say so at the interview. This should not affect whether or not you are offered the job, but it gives the office the opportunity to make proper arrangements – although 'special' treatment can sometimes be a delicate matter.

Accepting or Rejecting a Job

If you have not heard from the office within a week or ten days, write to remind them you are still interested in the job and ask when they will let you know. Telephoning is not a good idea – you may phone at an inconvenient moment or speak to the wrong person.

If they write to offer you a job, check that it states the terms correctly (in the light of what you were led to believe at the interview). It should state:

• the job title;
• where you will be working;
• the salary, when you will be paid and when the salaries are reviewed;

- the period of notice required on either side;
- arrangements for holidays and sick-leave;
- the date when you will start and when you will leave.

Never accept a job without a written statement along these lines, especially if you are going to work abroad.

Answer their letter promptly and confirm all the contents. This then forms a contract between you and the office, so you cannot then change your mind if, for example, another office turns up with a better offer. If you have any queries, get them sorted out before you write back. You might even visit the office again and talk to the person you will be working for – your 'boss'.

If you are waiting to hear the result of another interview, and receive an offer from one office, you can phone them and tell them that you are waiting to hear from someone else, and ask if they are prepared to keep their offer open. They may specify a date by when they must have your decision, one way or the other. You should not keep offices 'hanging on' – it is not good practice professionally and it may jeopardise the chances of a job being offered to another student, as well as causing some resentment towards what may be misinterpreted as a casual or cavalier attitude.

Accepting a Job
Once you have accepted a job write immediately to all the other offices with whom you have been dealing, and tell them politely that you are no longer interested. This may then free a vacancy for another student.

Rejecting a Job
If you feel that you must reject the offer of the job, write a polite letter back, as soon as possible. You don't have to go into any detail about the reasons. Similarly, if an office writes to reject your application, it is unlikely to tell you the reasons why and, since it may be to do with the business situation in the office as a whole, you should try not to take it personally.

3

At the Office

Your Year Out is the biggest change in your student life so far. Life in school and college has followed a set pattern with a certain amount of freedom, particularly in college. But an office is quite different. You are now being paid for the first time to do something responsibly; you are an essential part of an involved organisation, starting to give back something of what you have learned.

Offices have different atmospheres. Some can be strangely relaxed at times, at other times alarmingly frantic with panic. It may feel very empty when people are at meetings or on site visits. Realise that everyone else in the office has a business relationship with those around them, in terms of responsibility, authority, etc. Be patient. It may all seem either an anticlimax or rather daunting to start with. You may feel lonely, you may even be teased (watch out for the 'practical joker'!) – but try to keep a sense of humour and not take offence.

Settling in can take time, and it varies for different people. The day you come may not coincide with a convenient break for other staff to spare much time to start you into a job, so you may deliberately be given something simple to keep you occupied. This may be very simple and straightforward, but it will show how you can cope or draw, so

don't take it too lightly. Alternatively, the office may have something lined up for you to start on straight away.

The First Day
You should already have an idea of what you should wear, but if the office plan to take you on a visit on your first day to a building site, to show you the building you will be working on, appropriate clothing might be necessary.

If you will be using drawing boards you should take with you your own drawing instruments and scales, and possibly a set-square, although many offices now have drawing machines. If using CAD, it may be advisable to take a software manual that you normally find helpful. A pocket calculator may be useful. The office should provide 'consumables' – paper, pencils, ink, erasers, etc.

You should take any relevant income tax forms, such as form P45 if you have one from a previous employer. If you are starting work for the first time, your employer should provide a form P46 for your completion. At the end of the tax year (April) you will receive a form P60, recording the salary paid to you and deductions made at source; keep this carefully, as a duplicate cannot be issued if you lose it. Also take your National Insurance card, your medical card, and the name and address of your bank, with your account number and the bank's sort code (all in your cheque-book). If you are from overseas, you may need to take a work permit.

Catering Arrangements

Should you take your own lunch, or does everyone go out at lunch time and if so where? Is there a staff canteen or local pub? Does the office provide luncheon vouchers? Some offices ask you to provide your own tea cup or mug!

The Tour

You may be given a tour of the building (keep an eye open for the location of the toilets!) and be introduced to, probably, far too many people. Look out particularly for other students working elsewhere in the office, where printing takes place and where the office information or library is located. A secretary can be a useful ally and should be able to answer questions about the office routine if your boss is busy.

Meeting Colleagues

Others in the office will probably know nothing about you, and might not even know that you are coming. They may not want to ask you too much about yourself too soon, and may find your presence a little awkward to start with. You may be the first student they have taken on and they may be equally apprehensive. Some of the staff may be uncertain how to react to you, as well as you to them.

You may not be sure of the limits of your responsibility. This is most difficult to grasp initially. Your relationship with technicians in the office can be complicated. They may be younger, but will know more technically about construction than you and may be paid differently – or they may be much older, and have strong feelings about the value of qualifications and the remoteness of academic training from the practical realities of building. Never adopt a superior attitude or thrust your 'qualifications' at any one. It is better to ask questions intelligently, to listen and learn, adopting a relaxed and friendly approach wherever possible.

When people give you something to do, make sure that you know their name, where in the office they are working, and when they want the job done by. They may disappear and you will not know if it is wanted that same day or next week. In a small practice there may be no-one to ask if the boss goes out. This may be difficult to start with, but for many it can ultimately be rewarding, since you will gradually create your own position of authority.

Receiving Instructions

Be quite clear who is in charge of the work you do. Make sure you have a specific person to answer to, especially if you are in a team. You may be doing one job and someone may come along and ask you to do another, possibly claiming that it is more urgent. You should then check with the first person whether or not it is in order to switch tasks.

Try to identify what specifically you are being asked to do, make notes as you are being told so that you understand everything, and have a record to refer to. Get all the facts you need right at the start, and don't assume that the person will always be there to help later. He or she may be away for hours on site or in a meeting. Other people may be very busy and not have time to explain everything, but they should understand that they must allow time for you at this stage, otherwise they themselves will lose more time in having to re-do or re-explain your task.

Make sure you know what the drawing is required for, who needs it, and when it is required by. They may not think to explain the overall timetable for the job and just where your contribution will fit in. Again, ask to be put fully in the picture. Don't be tempted to do more by way of artistic elaboration once all the information necessary to convey the message is clearly down in the drawing.

You might be 'over-instructed' to begin with, but just bear with it, and don't complain. Remember the office does not know how much you know already. They may use office 'jargon', or other unfamiliar terminology, and may unthinkingly assume that you already know their standard ways and habits. Ask what it all means.

Instructions may also come as phone calls or letters, not necessarily connected with your particular job. Note the name, address, date and time when you receive the call and make sure it is passed on immediately – it may be more important than you think. Never assume you will remember and be able to deal with it when you have finished whatever you are doing. In a

small office, if the boss is away a good deal, communication may have to rely on written notes or phone calls.

You may be tempted to 'improve' a design or change a detail but don't do so until you have checked with your boss, or have been in the office long enough to understand their attitude and approach in such cases. If, however, you see what is an obvious inconsistency between one drawing and another, don't leave it, check with someone and, if agreed, correct it, but at the same time remember that it may have hidden consequences, and other drawings or documents may need to be corrected as well. The change should be recorded with the date and appropriate reference number. This is the critical area between being intelligent, constructive and useful to everyone, and being thoughtless, interfering and counter productive.

Finding Out
You will be expected to do much of this yourself, although in a very large office, which employs a full-time librarian, much of the preliminary work may already be done.

Office libraries vary enormously. A big office may have a fully stocked, up to date collection of information using computer-based systems, under the full-time control of a librarian. Medium-sized offices may rely on a member of staff to keep an eye open for relevant technical information and to build up the library, requesting information and filing it under an appropriate classification system. It is worthwhile getting familiar with the office library as soon as you can.

Some offices use the *Barbour Index* or the *RIBA Office Library Service* – commercial information companies who regularly visit the office to up-date the collection – but these systems do not necessarily include every item of relevant technical literature since they rely on the manufacturers of products for their co-operation.

There are various standard catalogues that contain much technical information, as well as commercial advertisement pages, and there are various card index systems.

All technical information should come with a CI/SfB classification code number *(see Glossary)* for filing, but some offices still persist in operating their own idiosyncratic system, the logic of which is lost in the past history of the office. The worst, however, is no system at all. Some offices, particularly the smaller ones, operate on the basis that when they want information they simply phone the manufacturer or supplier for the latest details.

You may wish to start to build up your own private collection of information, and this will certainly come in useful when you return to college, but many offices object to this practice because it can cause confusion in the office, so ask what the policy is.

The filing of correspondence and drawings rarely follows any standard pattern (there isn't one) and most offices seem to have invented their own

systems, so you should familiarise yourself with them as soon as you can. Spend any spare time reading the back history of jobs in the letter files.

Quality Assurance or Total Quality Management
Some offices have what might appear at first sight to be a bureaucratic system for issuing equipment, etc., using requisition slips or duplicate pads with countersigning by a higher authority. Effective management, sometimes called Quality Assurance or Total Quality Management, is becoming increasingly important for architectural practices and such arrangements may stem from these requirements – so ask what is expected of you in this respect.

Day-to-Day Working
You are a visible sign of the office's image and your chances of being invited to attend a meeting with a client or consultant will improve if you dress appropriately!

The way of addressing people is also relevant here. It depends on how long and how well you know them, but 'Sir' is no longer expected! Wait and see how they address each other. On the other hand, do not be too informal, especially to begin with, because it may sound cheeky and out of place. Avoid over familiarity when talking to the contractor, or you may not have the respect you expected.

When working by yourself, never do anything you cannot explain confidently and justify subsequently to others, or anything beyond your capabilities.

Don't fudge things or make things up. If you come to a standstill, waiting for work to be checked, explore the rest of the drawings or the history of the job in the files rather than just sitting there.

Aspects of building science, such as calculating daylight factors or heat loss, and up to date legislation and contracts are things which you are probably better at doing and know more about since you are more familiar with them from your recent academic studies than some practitioners, who may only do such things at infrequent intervals. Equally, you will be expected to know the fundamentals of surveying, so brush up on all these skills if necessary.

Working in a Group
This will not be the same as working in a group at college, where you all have a similar age and position in the educational system, but it will involve working with people of different ages and from a wide range of different backgrounds. If there is a conflict of opinion you may not know if it is wise to speak out, possibly against those who are supposed to know better than you.

Understanding the line and span of control is very important, particularly in a large office organisation. Is it a flat pyramid with one partner in overall charge, or a steeper pyramid with a number of equal partners sharing the responsibility? Is it arranged in teams or groups based on the particular job or contract, or teams based on particular aspects of work with various specialisms or concentrations, so that only a few can see the overall picture?

Understanding Office 'Customs'
Many offices have an 'Office Manual' which covers these day-to-day practices. Read it carefully and abide by its rules. The office may have specific drawing techniques which you are not used to or positively dislike, or you may be left entirely to your own devices and not be sure what thickness of pen nib to use. Who makes the tea? Understand the filing system for drawings and letters.

Does the office have a fire drill? You are working in an inflammable situation! Where are the fire exits and fire extinguishers? Is there a First Aid box to hand? What would happen if there was an injury or sudden illness?

Time Keeping
Regular time-keeping is a novelty for students. Getting used to a seven or eight hour day, five days a week, may be difficult at first. Don't be late or let yourself get behind. Understand the value of good time keeping to the office, the reflected image of efficiency on your part if you are good at it, and the problems it can cause when people abuse it.

Time-keeping is important because it is a record of the time spent on a job. It is used for costing the job and for charging the client. The fee income, viability and profitability of the office will depend on this, so fill in your daily time-sheets accurately as you go along. Punctuality implies a degree of discipline inherent in a well-run office. It is a business and it must be efficient. Someone must be there to deal with the first call of the day, which may be from a new client, and if there is no reply he or she will go elsewhere.

Some offices operate 'flexi-time'. Under this system you work the same number of hours but the starting and finishing times vary within the working day. If the office is on 'flexi-time', you will need to adjust to it carefully. Not everyone in these offices may be allowed to work 'flexi-time', and abuse of the system can lead to unpleasantness, for example, when some staff appear to have rather long lunch 'hours'.

Time off from work is strictly restricted (except under very special circumstances). You are limited to a specific number of holiday days, and no more, so these are valuable. Plan your holiday periods carefully, discuss them with your boss and give plenty of notice if you can beforehand so that others can fill in for you. Send the office a postcard from your exotic holiday island!

Time off should be allowed by the office for specific visits and events in connection with your practical training.

If you are away ill or on holiday, try and make sure beforehand that someone knows where your current work is, so that someone else can carry on with it if necessary.

You must always get your work checked over. There should be no embarrassment or publicity of your 'ignorance' when you do this. If you think that you have made a mistake, don't be afraid to own up. Everyone makes mistakes, particularly in the first few weeks, and it is rarely as catastrophic as you might think, but whatever you do, don't try to fudge or cover it up. It provides the opportunity for others to help and to deal with any repercussions.

If you are asked to do something that you believe to be technically incorrect, gently point out that you are puzzled and explain why. If still asked to do it that way, you must grit you teeth (silently!) and proceed to do it. You have to assume that 'they know better than you' and that you are there to learn, despite what you feel to the contrary.

If you are asked to do something that you believe to be morally or ethically wrong, it is more difficult. You could tactfully explain your view and ask to be excused from that particular piece of work, but here the final decision must be yours.

If you are offered gifts, or what appears to be an 'inducement' of any sort – even the traditional bottle of whisky at Christmas from someone outside of the office – it may be misunderstood as a bribe or inducement and as such is not acceptable in terms of your strict professional behaviour. It is always best to say, 'no thank you', difficult as that may be. You will then never be compromised.

Organising Yourself
Get into the habit of always thinking and planning ahead. Use your office diary positively for your own benefit and to help others.

There are two organisational programmes, your own internal one and the external one into which you fit. The external programme may be largely done for you; your problem will be organising your internal programme to match. If the external one is not done for you, you have the extra burden of doing it yourself and it must take precedence over your own. You cannot work in isolation, but you will always have to relate to larger programmes around you. Make sure, therefore, you know your boss's programme as well as your own. If you are doing work for a variety of people, perhaps in different offices, they won't necessarily appreciate your problems or your priorities, and this will need careful handling on your part.

Understanding the time-scale within which your work is required to be finished may be an initial problem. When asked how long something will take you, it may be impossible for you to say with any accuracy since you will have had no previous experience. As soon as you can – and, better still, in your studio work in college – try to develop time management skills by timing yourself, to see how long it takes, roughly, to do certain types of drawings. Make a record for future reference. It is very important to be able to deliver the goods on time, so this ability to time and pace yourself needs to be learnt.

Try and ask how much time is allowed overall for each job, see how everybody relates to that and where your particular contribution comes in. How critical is that timing and what are the financial and wider programming implications? Is there a 'critical path' through the programme? Can you see ways in which that could be achieved more efficiently?

Try and broaden your general interest in architecture outside office hours, by attending meetings of the local architectural society, visiting exhibitions, and by some background reading carried out in your own time.

Relationships Within the Office

In some very large organisations you may never (or only rarely) meet senior people in charge of the office. They may not appear to take an interest in you or your work. Whilst unfortunately this is to some degree inevitable, it may be up to you to make yourself known to them from time to time, by expressing an interest in, say, the overall work of the office.

With your 'boss', the person you are immediately responsible to for your day-to-day work, various problems may occur. He or she may expect a higher standard of work than you can do at your level, and when the inevitable mistake happens, little understanding or sympathy may be shown. On the other hand, your capabilities and work capacity may not be appreciated and you may be treated with an over-controlling or a patronising attitude.

Some students find it difficult if their 'boss' is frequently out of the office or does not appear to be working as hard as they are, but you should understand that he or she may have a number of legitimate activities, related to the work but unknown to you, which take him/her out of the office. You may find it a little awkward at first if your boss is in the same room as yourself, since you may sense the tension of being under constant supervision and feel unable to relax. These are examples of the factors that might produce some initial stress, but they have to be overcome – just recognising them as part of the office 'psychology' is half the battle.

You are a member of a team, but the boundaries of authority between the various members may be unclear and this may cause problems. Insufficient information may be given to you about who else is working on the same job as yourself, or what other jobs they are on, and this might lead to misunderstandings. There is also the danger of you being 'Man Friday' – passed around according to need – so you never feel fully involved or responsible and never see anything you do followed through to its end.

It may be difficult for you to know what attitude to adopt to others in the office since you will not understand the relative power structure involved. Being the most junior can sometimes be awkward, perhaps because you are seen by others to have the least responsibility and so you may be 'put upon'. Do you get used as a 'scapegoat'? Do you always get sent to deal with the persistent visits from unpopular representatives of firms selling equipment or materials? You may become aware of 'groupings' within the office, not related to teams nor related to projects, and there may be friction between such groups. Whose side should you be on, and can you afford to remain independent?

With ancillary and administrative staff, always show the same consideration that you yourself would expect to receive. You may find that support staff seem to work for themselves, or establish their own priorities, which do not accord with those of the office and certainly not with yours. Be patient and understand the sometimes routine nature of their work and why they feel the need for a show of independence from time to time. Secretaries are often the ones with the real 'power' in the office, so it is worth understanding their role and working helpfully with them. Don't forget that politeness will often get a letter done quickly!

Learn the relationships with outside consultants and contractors. Perhaps the least tangible role is that of the Clerk of Works whose position and authority you must understand. Normally appointed and paid by the client, the Clerk of Works is not a member of the contractor's organisation and therefore has, to some extent, an independent position on the building site. You can learn much from a good Clerk of Works, so try to establish a good relationship from the outset.

The Unions will probably not affect you, but you should be aware of their existence if you work in a local government or similar type of office.

Asking for a rise. Dates of salary reviews should have been included in your letter of appointment, but if they were not, and if you have not heard anything after six months, it might be worth asking – not bluntly, but for a general discussion on your progress. If the atmosphere seems right, ask about when you might be considered for an increase.

Some General Comments

- Speak slowly and clearly when you introduce yourself or other people to each other, discover the correct 'etiquette' and remember to state their role or position in the job.

- You may come across people who say that academic qualifications are of no real use, and that you are wasting your time at college. Don't be provoked into an argument over this.

- You are in a position of trust, as a professional with the appropriate level of behaviour, but you should not be put in the position of having to admonish anyone, condemn, or order alterations to work done on the site. You have no authority to do this.

- Too much talk wastes time and money, so don't become a chatterbox or the office 'gossip'. You might get your fingers burnt! If told something in confidence, keep it so. It is wise to avoid political or religious discussions, particularly in your early days in the office.

- Not everyone in the office organisation will be on an 'even

keel'. There are stresses, jealousies, friendships, enemies, etc. People often behave differently when at work than when at home. Some work diligently from '9 to 5' and then switch off, some take work home with them, and some become 'workaholics'. Some offices may expect the student to bring in a breath of fresh air – not necessarily architectural! – so welcome that opportunity.

If you find that you are having difficulties working in the office, don't panic, try and stick with it initially. Put the problem into context, and decide how long to give it to clear itself. You may be over expectant and a time for reflection may resolve the matter. Why aren't you happy? Is it the type of work, poor pay, or the people you are with? Are you stuck on one job, is it repetitive, or are you bullied or teased? Is there too much bureaucracy, or is there altogether too much chaos around you? But don't be hasty and don't resign in a fit of pique. If nothing else, moving job after a short time without proper consultation is very bad practice.

If the problem does not clear in a few days, first talk to your boss, who may well be aware of the difficulty and may reassure you that it is being resolved. If it lasts longer, go back to your boss and also let the Practical Training Adviser at your school know your predicament. He or she should be able to help by mutual discussion. If it still doesn't work out and you want to leave, then do so only with the advice and knowledge of your Practical Training Adviser.

How to Succeed!

- Seize all opportunities to demonstrate your ability to work.
- Tackle all mundane jobs with efficiency and enthusiasm.
- Ask if you don't understand anything.
- Co-operate – try and help your colleagues.
- Anticipate problems, and tactfully make suggestions for improvements.
- Never blame others for YOUR mistakes.
- Never blame others for THEIR mistakes.
- Do not gossip.
- Do not 'creep'.
- Maintain politeness, courtesy, tact and, above all, a sense of humour.

4

Office Ways and Methods

Drawings

Drawings are a means to an end, and not an end in themselves. You are no longer doing drawings to impress examiners or tutors in a school of architecture, but for clients, other consultants, planners, specialist subcontractors or for the builders in huts on rain soaked muddy sites in winter.

The office may dictate the medium and general style of drawing, as part of their policy and house 'style', and many work largely with computer-aided design (CAD). The use of CAD is becoming more and more widespread, but the number of different methods and approaches for using CAD are just as broad. Remember though that CAD's benefits are numerous, such as: layering of information; the ease at which designs/drawings can be amended; the ease at which CAD drawings can be sent to other people in the team; the effective handling of 2-D and 3-D shapes; etc. However, always remember that there will be a house 'style'.

Is a drawing to be 'pictorial' or 'diagrammatic'? In most cases the approach is likely to be 'diagrammatic' or 'mechanical' and there is rarely room for demonstrating your 'artistic' flair, except perhaps for the occasional presentation perspective. Even then the office usually has someone who

specialises in these. 'Diagrammatic' drawings are often exploratory sketch drawings, usually to scale; 'mechanical' drawings are the more conventional working drawings, always to scale.

Speed is of the essence and you may find that accuracy decreases the faster you draw, so take care. You may find yourself going from the rough sketch to the finished detail all on the same piece of tracing paper. Plan the organisation of your drawing on the paper beforehand so that you don't leave excessive 'white' space on the paper.

Don't draw anything you don't understand. Don't make it up and don't make assumptions. Know what is essential to put in and what to leave out. Don't waste time hatching in acres of paper. Consider the sequence of how the thing is to be built. It may be an idea to do explanatory or cut-away drawings showing the stages in construction and erection, just for your own understanding at first, and then as drawings for others to follow. If you don't know how the thing is to be made or built, nobody else will.

The term 'negative' is generally used in offices. It does not mean a negative in the photographic sense. It is a 'positive' drawing on tracing paper from which any number of copies can be printed on special paper.

It is essential to develop a good clear style of freehand lettering (you should have been doing this all the way through college anyway), but don't start doing anything 'fancy' with swirls and flourishes, in the office. A sheet of graph paper permanently placed on your drawing board as a backing sheet provides a constant set of parallel guide lines and spaces. Stencilling, with special ink pens following the letters pre-cut in plastic strips needs practice, particularly in getting spacing right. Find time, preferably in your own time, to practise. The office may also use 'Transtext', typing on adhesive transparent tape. Ironically, 'Letraset', the one system you probably know best, is expensive, slow and may be used only rarely.

Office procedures for drawing numbering must be followed, even if it seems odd to you. There is usually a good reason for it. Some systems relate to the sequence of component, location and assembly, using the CI/SfB numbers or the UNICLASS system, with a system of numbers to cross-reference between drawings. There are offices that still use a simple sequence of numbering each consecutive drawing, but in others CPI (Co-ordinated Project Information) is adopted. Some architects have their own standard details that they will not willingly relinquish. If you are working under different people at the same time this may be awkward and difficult to reconcile without confrontation.

Get your drawing checked at interim stages rather than when you think you have finished it. You may have to make revisions to drawings done by others, so always consider how your amendments may affect other parts of the same drawing and generally think of the consequences of alterations. Note carefully the way of recording revisions on drawings (sometimes a letter code is affixed to the drawing number), the date (most important), and a brief summary of the alterations, in a column on one side of the drawing. There are many different ways of making corrections. One is 'cut and paste', drawing out the correction and then sticking it onto the original for printing. The most difficult is altering an ink drawing, using a razor blade and/or erasers, which tend to leave a rough surface on which to draw revisions. A useful tip is to burnish the affected area with your fingernail to restore a smooth surface. Overlay drafting allows the superimposition of up to, say, six negatives which can be accurately aligned in order to compose a particular arrangement of information.

Printing Processes

Get to know whoever operates the office print machine, or whether the office prefers to use the printing firm round the corner. These people can be a useful ally. If the machine is in your office get to know how it works because you may have to step in and use it at short notice sometime. Make sure the print order is clear, not only how many but what type, and find out beforehand who or what they are for. Get familiar with Xerox or similar machines. Find out what they can do by way of enlargements or reductions to scale. If enlarging or reducing a drawing, make sure it has a graphic scale drawn on it first.

Model Making

There may be occasions when you might be asked to make a model. Large presentation models are usually produced by outside specialist firms, but the student is often seen as someone who has recent experience of model-making in college and the necessary dexterity to produce a reasonable model. Rather as with drawings, understand for whom the model is intended and make it accordingly. You will have to be quick and accurate, but making simple explanatory models to help at the design stage is a very useful skill. Make sure they are photographed (for your own records as well), before they inevitably disintegrate.

Writing

You may be expected to write your own letters. Always get them checked, not just for 'English' or spelling, but to ensure that they say what you intend and are free from ambiguity. This action also implies confirmation by someone in authority who will take responsibility for them initially. This applies even for simple requests for trade literature.

The office may have standard letters with a preferred layout and style. Look on the letter files to see copies of normal office practice and don't try to be 'original'.

Draft the letter so you can alter it easily. You may be expected to deal with your own typing of letters and reports – particularly in smaller, younger

practices. If working on handwritten drafts, make sure your handwriting is clear, and don't abbreviate words on the assumption that a typist will recognise them and expand them back to their original length. Don't write more than is necessary, keep it all simple and straight to the point. Use short sentences and avoid longwinded 'conventions', e.g. 'I am in receipt of yours of the 14th inst.' – just say, 'Thank you for your letter of July 14th ...'. Check if the office uses the first person singular (I), first person plural (We), or, rarely, the impersonal third person singular (It).

At the head of every letter always quote the job name, its reference number, the date and refer to any previous letter. This eases referencing, ensures that there are no gaps in the sequence of correspondence and that no letter remains unanswered. State the purpose of the letter clearly and in the most straightforward manner. Don't try to be funny or clever. Your letter may be read in a court of law at some later date.

Get someone in authority to check the draft. Some partners may change letters for no apparent reason. Don't feel insulted. It may not be intended as a reflection on you, but to maintain a consistent office image. Nevertheless, ask why it has been changed.

Always check every letter when it comes back from typing and before it goes to be signed and posted. Typists can make mistakes, so don't be bemused by the professional printed appearance of the typed letter. If there are mistakes it is not too difficult to get it changed. Secretaries usually don't read through what they have typed, and may not always understand what you are saying anyway. Sometimes they can miss out a whole line when an interruption, a phone call perhaps, can 'throw' them off course. A good typist, however, might helpfully point out an apparent error in your draft. Dictating to typists is a skill which you would not be expected to have at this stage, although you might experiment with a dictating machine if the office uses them.

In most offices every letter is seen and signed by the partner (or equivalent) in charge. Never sign your name only. If you are allowed to sign, then sign your name followed by the words 'for and on behalf of' (then the name of the office, or of the head of the office).

A copy of EVERY letter MUST be kept on file. It is tempting to keep copies for yourself as well as the obligatory copy on the office file. But you are advised not to do this since such copies may get into the wrong hands, besides causing clutter and confusion. However, if copies would be of value to you in your later school studies or a case study required for the Examination in Professional Practice, obtain the permission of the writer of the letter, your boss and senior partner before taking a copy.

Compliment slips are frequently used to accompany, for example, a set of drawings when they are sent out and no explanatory letter is thought to be necessary. This is not wise practice, but even so they should have on them exactly what is being sent, and a copy must go on the file as record of what has been sent to whom and when. A normal covering letter, listing what is going, is better practice – and a copy is automatically kept on file.

In larger offices, inter-departmental memos vary according to the conventions of the office. They often take the form of duplicate or triplicate pads, sometimes referred to as 'ping-pongs', with tear out returnable pages that can be used to confirm both sides of a decision.

If a letter is likely to run to more than two pages it may be worth writing it in the form of a *report*. Again, see if the office has a standard format for report writing.

A report is not an essay. It is principally factual, keeping to the essential points, and written to suit the recipient. The personal present tenses are normally avoided in report writing, usually the third person perfect or other past tense is used, e.g. 'It has been noted that, etc.'.

Be brief, don't repeat anything, keep the items in order, compose it in relatively short paragraphs related to one topic at a time, with a sub-heading, and use cross-referencing between the numbered paragraphs. Use key words and underline or highlight the most important matters. Use diagrams and sketches if appropriate rather than lengthy verbal descriptions. Double spacing between lines and ample margins, giving room for the recipient to add his comments, are of benefit. There might be an 'action' column alongside, indicating who should be responding to that particular item – but the danger of that is that the reader will only look for the part which concerns him and may miss the overall message of the report.

Specification writing is not usually taught to any extent in schools of architecture in the early years, but the office may expect you to attempt a simple piece of specification writing. The advice is to look once again at previous examples done in the office.

Telephones and Other Equipment
When making outgoing calls have the number ready with the name of the person you want to speak to, plus an alternative name should he or she not be available. Assemble all relevant information beforehand, in order, including drawings, scale and file of letters. State your query or request precisely. For example, ask for information, with costs and dates, and when you need the information by.

You may find it difficult to describe a building, or more particularly, parts of a building, over the phone. Up to now you will have always spoken about these things 'eye-to-eye' at criticisms etc., with the drawings available to point at. On the 'phone you will need more patience and good control to guide someone else through a drawing by 'remote' control.

When receiving calls, don't say just 'hello' – give the name of the firm and say who you are. Ask who is speaking and from which organisation. Ask for his or her phone number in case you are cut off or need to return the call later. Have a standard message pad always by the phone, with a pencil to hand! Ask to whom he or she wishes to speak and in connection with which job. If that person is not available ask if you can take a message.

Note the time and date, the name of the job, details of the message and when the caller can be contacted in return. Make sure the message is taken by you to the person for whom it is intended immediately you have put down the receiver. If you are out when a call comes for you and a message awaits you, call back promptly.

Some General Comments

• If there is an office ruling on personal calls get this clear at the outset.

• In a small office don't sit too near the phone or you will become the telephone receptionist. If there is a separate telephonist it is worth getting to know them early on.

• Recordings on dictaphones need to be accurate, without breaks and changes of mind! Dictaphones can save time. Some find them fun, others find them very intimidating.

• Small offices often use a telephone answering machine.

• Fax machines and e-mail are becoming standard for transmitting letters and documents.

Computers are increasingly used in offices, and as a student you may be expected to be more up to date and more efficient than some of the older staff in the office. Some larger offices make good use of computers, but some offices bought inappropriate systems for prestigious reasons and now rather regret having done so. Some offices have found too much time is spent on programming or having to wait for a technical expert – sometimes one stage removed from the work and not conversant with the architectural problem. If you have had computer experience in college you may be able to be of great value here.

Meeting Visitors
There will be visitors to the office, official and unofficial, invited or uninvited. *Consultants* working on projects may include structural engineers, quantity surveyors, lighting and heating consultants or specialists such as commercial kitchen designers. They are usually invited to the office (though equally you may go to their offices at times) and good co-operation with them is essential. *Technical experts or representatives* from manufacturers of building components may also be invited, such as a manufacturer of a patent glazing system. All these people are very valuable to the office, and often long-standing relationships have been built up over the years, and you, in turn, will be able to learn much from them.

Quantity surveyors have traditionally been cast as the most difficult people to satisfy, since they apparently act as dampeners to architects' wilder flights of enthusiasm. In fact, the architect should always be in control of costs when designing. A good quantity surveyor is a great asset here, with an ability to monitor costs and to anticipate the financial consequences of various decisions. Seeing how quantity surveyors work may be the most important lesson you will learn from your time in an office, so make a point of getting on with them and make every effort to see the value of their contribution, and to 'talk their language'.

You may be invited to attend meetings with other people outside the office. Such meetings will more usually be held at their offices rather than your own, such as those of the *building contractors*, the *planning officers*, the *building control officers*, the *fire officers*, and maybe the *client*. You may also attend meetings with *community groups* to explain your scheme. This can be a most testing occasion, since you will have to explain your ideas to laymen in non-technical language, with much tact, understanding and sympathy. Some residents in housing estates, or others controlled by a form of invisible and absent bureaucracy may find in the architect someone at last to complain to about everything.

Representatives of firms who just 'drop in' in an attempt to sell you their particular products are perhaps the people you will meet most frequently, and sometimes they may be the most difficult to handle. It is hard to resist a barrage of sales talk – their skill at selling is their livelihood. Say that you only have five minutes, and try and ask the following:

(a) Has the product been used elsewhere, by whom, when, and can it be seen in use?

(b) What is the life span, what maintenance is required, is replacement practical, is it easy to fix, and are spare parts available?

(c) Does it conform to any British or International Standards, or has it an Agrément Certificate?

(d) About costs – initial and maintenance, delivery times, and whether you can be given samples, as well as the trade literature.

Prevent representatives from prying into other projects that may be at a confidential stage in the office. Representatives are often on the look-out for opportunities to move in and be first on something new! Try not to be confounded or confused by sales talk of a pseudo-scientific nature. Don't be frightened by the 'rep', remember his or her whole job is basically to sell something, so if you're not sure, don't feel pressurised. Beware of having lunch with them. Learn the gentle art of bluff. Many representatives are, in fact, very helpful. It pays them to be helpful, because you may specify their product or call on them again in your future career. Therefore keep a list of the names, addresses and phone numbers of all these people you meet, for your own records. You may want to get back to them again at a later date.

Meetings
You will encounter various types of meetings, and they will differ considerably. Within the office there may be regular *staff meetings* to discuss or report on overall office policy, or *group or team meetings* to discuss the progress of certain jobs, or short *presentations to the assembled office of a new design project* followed by a discussion, rather like reviews or criticism sessions in school.

You should try and attend all relevant meetings whenever possible. Ask to be taken. Appreciate the value of informal meetings with planners, building control officers and fire officers, in helping to resolve any problems prior to the submission of the applications for official approval. Before attending such meetings check the actual documents so that you know what information you will need to take with you. If you don't understand the reasons for the sort of questions raised, ask the persons involved to explain.

Establish what form of travel you are expected to use if you are asked to travel to outside meetings and how you will be reimbursed. If asked to use your own car on office business check your insurance company will cover this. It usually means paying an extra premium. The office should pay this and should have a recognised rate of reimbursement to cover petrol and mileage. Get VAT receipts for all purchases and submit them with your claim.

Proper briefing before a meeting is essential: Questions to ask include:

- What is the meeting for?
- When is it?
- Who will be coming?
- How long should it last?
- Why are they coming?
- Is it one of an established series, or the first of its type?

An agenda is essential for most meetings. It should be sent out in good time to all attending. It should indicate the major as opposed to minor items that will be discussed.

Before the meeting itself read all relevant files, study all relevant drawings and ask about them if you have any doubts or queries. You should not question your own office's drawings during a meeting with outsiders.

If invited to attend a meeting as an observer see who runs the meeting. If it is your boss you might be able to help (and learn) by producing parallel notes for writing-up later back in the office. Try to identify the priorities from the irrelevancies, work out who is who and their roles and ensure that all names are recorded accurately, even if you have to ask more than once! It is unlikely you will be required to run a meeting on your own to start with, but you might have to step in at short notice. In that case, it is important your boss knows you are going and has confirmed just exactly how much authority you will actually have.

The course of the meeting should follow this pattern:

(a) *Introductions.* Make sure everyone knows who everyone is, what they do and why they are there.

(b) *Previous minutes* (which should have already been circulated). Are they a true record or do they need amendment for the sake of correctness of the record? Once agreed, they should be signed and dated there and then.

(c) *Matters arising from those minutes.* Identify and follow up everything by rapidly going through the previous minutes to check everything has been covered or to report on any subsequent developments.

(d) *Current agenda.* This is the list of the main matters of the present meeting.

(e) *The date, time and place of next meeting.*

In your own notes, highlight the matters to follow up as soon as you report back to the office. It is absolutely essential one person is in control of a meeting and that everyone recognises his or her role. He or she has to give everyone a chance to speak in turn, to cut someone short if necessary, to bring someone in who may be eager or reluctant to speak, to sum up the point reached and to move the meeting along according to the agenda.

The 'Minutes' are 'an official record of the proceedings of a meeting'.

Usually a Minute is a short note or memorandum, recording a particular point or decision. It is not a fully detailed account of everything that was said prior to that conclusion or decision. Minutes are only 'valid' if they are agreed and signed as a true record at a subsequent meeting. They should be written up, checked, typed and distributed as soon as possible after the meeting and not sent out weeks later with the agenda for the next meeting.

Record the names and positions of all those present at the meeting (and the time if anyone left before the end), as well as the date, time and place. Itemise everything in short, numbered paragraphs, each one relating to one topic at a time. Be concise. An 'action column' is usually added alongside. Add a distribution list on the minutes so that everyone can see who else has received a copy, as well as identifying the number of copies required and who they should go to.

It is difficult at times to concentrate and identify the key matters and decisions. Some form of fast note taking, your own 'speedwriting' might be an idea, but it can sometimes be very difficult to unravel it all back in the office, and certainly don't give any such abbreviated notes to a typist.

Site Visits
- Try to use these 'educationally', by preparing yourself beforehand, if you can, by reading through the files and studying the drawings related to the job.
- Always tell the site agent you are on the site as you enter.
- Never instruct any workmen directly.
- Look out for things which interest you – a detail on a drawing, for example, and then go and see how it has actually turned out in

practice. Even though it may not be part of the business of the meeting you are attending, you usually get a chance to look around.
- Take your camera (or sketch-book), but tell the site agent what you are doing and why – some contractors are suspicious of this and suspect espionage or photographic evidence that may be used against them in a later claim for damages or delay.
- Check you are covered by insurance when you are on the contractor's site, wear sensible tough clothing and a safety helmet at all times.
- Try using a pocket tape recorder for on site inspections, rather than a notebook and pencil.

5

Picking It Up as You Go!

Finance

This is probably the most difficult area, so you will probably have to ask for information in this area. It would take the office considerable time to explain it in any depth and most offices assume there is little point in explaining it to a student whose length of stay in the office is limited.

Cost controls operate constantly in all areas of the job and the office. Try to be aware of them and understand how they relate to your work. Everything you do will have a financial consequence.

The cost of the project depends on which stage the project has reached. At the early design stage estimates will exist for the overall cost, and it is particularly useful to try and identify the main areas of expense. There should be some form of cost plan, which will show the relative values of various elements of the building and how costs are allocated. All major design decisions at this stage are monitored in relation to the cost plan and estimate.

You are responsible for spending your client's money, not yours or the office's, and part of your total design responsibility is to design with costs firmly in mind all the time. You will begin to see how higher quality finishes or complex detailing may incur additional expenses, which either have to be compensated for by reductions elsewhere or sometimes sacrificed altogether. Whilst sometimes depressing, this is a hard and necessary lesson.

If you join the job after the contract has been let, start by carefully studying the priced bills of quantities. This will give you a clear idea of where the money is going. The relative cost of materials is a useful lesson to learn. A close check has to be kept at this stage on any alterations or delays to the job, and no changes should be considered without first reviewing the financial position. The role of the quantity surveyor is critical here.

Office Costs

The cost of running the office includes such items as rent of the premises, rates, insurance, heating and lighting, cleaning, etc., as well as staff salaries. Although not directly your responsibility, you should be aware of them, even if only to the extent of being economical in using paper and stationery and switching off unnecessary lights!

Staff Cost Money

How much do you cost the office? How much does the office charge the client for your time? It might not be possible to see a breakdown of the fees in this way, but students can be shocked to find that the office charges a particular amount per hour for them, a figure which might seem high in relation to the rate of pay. But remember there are hidden costs and office overheads to be covered.

Time

The importance of accurately completing time-sheets is worth re-stating. You should try and see how the information collected from them is handled in terms of calculating fees, covering overheads and even producing a profit. See how it is monitored in relation to the staff time costs estimated by the office. It might be useful to know how long you can stay on a particular job or part of a job without incurring additional costs to the overall job budget.

Your time should not be wasted. It is costing the office (and client) something, so always try to be constructive and positive in this direction. Use time to the best advantage of the office, and you will also benefit yourself. Identify an area where you could make a contribution, or see how and when you could tactfully suggest a possible improvement.

Legal

There are separate and distinct areas of legislation that affect all buildings. Before any building can commence, relevant approvals should have been received.

Planning Regulations

Approval for any development has to be granted under the various Town and Country Planning Acts. Although these are Acts passed by central government, they are administered by the local authority (the Town Hall) for the area

concerned. They will have all the necessary application forms and details of what drawings they require. If the planning officers are satisfied with the proposals, they will recommend to the Council's planning committee that approval be given.

Planning officers are professionals, advising the Planning Committee which is made up of locally elected non-expert lay people. The timing of the meetings of the Planning Committee may be critical and a month or longer delay may follow failure to submit at the right time for a particular meeting. The consequences of this for the overall job programme in the office are obvious, hence the last minute 'panics' that sometimes precede such submissions. Once again, informal contact with planning officials will help to avoid this and any other last minute hitches caused by minor 'technical' infringements. There are many other related matters, such as 'listed building consent' for alterations to historic buildings and for development in conservation areas.

Building Regulations

Building Regulations are even today still erroneously referred to by some as building 'bye-laws'. They are made under the Building Act and the details are set out in the Building Regulations. Their concern is with health (e.g. drainage); safety (e.g. structural design or stair design); aspects of the control of fire spread (e.g. how much window area you can have close to the site boundary); and many other matters, including energy conservation.

As with Planning Regulations, they are operated by a special division within the local authority in the Town Hall and submissions are required in the same way, but for different committee approval. Building Regulations are quite separate from Planning Regulations, and approval of the one in no way implies approval of the other. In London, certain aspects of the London Building Acts (outside the Building Regulations) may still apply, as does the more formal system of getting approval for alterations to 'party wall structures', which are shared walls on the boundary of two neighbouring properties. There are other matters such as *easements* – that is, getting permission to allow rights of way across other properties, perhaps for service or drainage access – many of which involve common rather than statute law.

Fire Regulations
There is a division of responsibility between the Building Control Officers (who administer the Building Regulations) and the Fire Authority (who operate under the Fire Precautions Act). The design and construction of buildings in respect of fire safety is the responsibility of the Building Control Officers in the local authorities, in consultation with the Fire Authority. Fire considerations in respect of the occupation and use of the buildings, however, is the province of the Fire Authority, under the Fire Precautions Act.

There are also many other pieces of legislation affecting buildings. For example, access for the disabled, the licensing of premises, and aspects of the Health and Safety at Work Act. There are special acts for cinemas and theatres, for factories and for the storage of hazardous materials, and there may be pieces of local legislation that are relevant. The list can be a very long one. Furthermore, there are matters of property law and tort which, though they are unlikely to affect you at this stage, will eventually form part of your studies.

Try to see the typical forms which accompany these submissions and how many copies of drawings should go with them. Do they need to be coloured up in any special way? What sort of fees are involved with submissions? It may be sensible to get your own copy of the Building Regulations, or one of the many excellent explanatory books (*see section on 'Further Reading'*). Some of this will be in advance of the stage you will have reached in your school course, but it is worth getting hold of as many of the standard documents as you can now, since you will need to refer to them in more detail in professional practice courses in later years at school.

In Scotland, building work is covered by the Building Standards (Scotland) Regulations. These differ substantially from the regulations applicable in England and Wales, particularly in matters of escape and access for the disabled, which are covered by the Scottish Standards Regulations.

The Construction (Design and Management) Regulations 1994
Under the CDM Regulations, clients, for the first time, have legal duties imposed on them when they initiate a

construction, maintenance or demolition project. Their obligations only end when the building is demolished or passed to a new owner. There are only three situations which exempt a project from these regulations:

(i) domestic projects (typically having one's dwelling built or maintained);

(ii) projects whose site work takes less than 31 days or 501 person days;

(iii) where there are less than five persons on site at any one time.

The client's key responsibilities are:

To appoint a competent Planning Supervisor and allow that person:

(i) adequate resources to do the job;

(ii) to contribute to the project's Health and Safety Plan;

(iii) to appoint competent Designers and a Principal Contractor and to allow those parties adequate resources to fulfil their obligations;

(iv) to ensure that construction does not start until the Health and Safety Plan is ready;

(v) to retain for future reference the Health and Safety File on completion of the project.

In practice a client may appoint the Planning Supervisor to undertake these duties. Failure to ensure the preparation of a Health and Safety Plan can result in civil action. Prosecutions concerning damages arising out of shortcomings in the Plan may result in actions being brought in the criminal courts by the Health and Safety Executive.

The Planning Supervisor's role is to administer the CDM regulations on behalf of the client, including:

(i) giving advice as to the competence of the Designers and Principal Contractor;

(ii) ensuring the preparation of the Health and Safety Plan;

(iii) ensuring the issue of the Health and Safety Plan to the contractors;

(iv) ensuring the preparation and deposit of the Health and Safety File with the client.

In considering whether to offer a Planning Supervisor service, architects should be aware of:

(i) the need for formal training, qualification, and accreditation;

(ii) the danger of a conflict of interest when also offering design services on the same project;

(iii) the legal and insurance implications.

The designers' responsibilities are:

(i) to avoid foreseeable risks to the health and safety of those working on the project;

(ii) to eliminate through design the chance of risk wherever possible;

(iii) to ensure design information makes explicit any health and safety risks within the design;

(iv) to provide information for the compilation of the Health and Safety Plan.

Architects are required to be conversant with the common causes of injury in the construction and maintenance of buildings; to become familiar with the legislation and guidance documentation surrounding the subject and to set up systematic risk assessment procedures, with regard to their design processes, in order to eliminate risk wherever possible.

Building Contracts

The topic of building contracts is extensive and complex, and it is not possible to describe here the various types of building contracts and their associated procedures in full. However, by reading through contract files in the office (and by referring to textbooks, *see section on 'Further Reading'*), you should get a general idea of how the contract operates in practice. All building contracts used in Scotland are subject to the laws of Scotland and include supplements to cover this.

It is important to understand that, in traditional terms, the architect's role in the project changes once the contract has been signed between the client and the contractor. Prior to this point the architect was solely responsible to the client, but hereafter it is now the architect's duty to apply the conditions of the contract with absolute fairness between the client and the contractor.

The architect is not usually expected to inspect constantly the erection of the building, but only to give 'periodical inspection'. If regular inspection is required a Clerk of Works will be employed by the client – not by the contractor or the architect. Inspection is the architect's duty; supervision is the contractor's duty.

The following terms and expressions, arranged roughly according to the sequence of operations, will be heard frequently in the office in connection with the contract:

Contract

An agreement or promise which the law recognises as binding on the parties to it. The contractor undertakes to carry out the Works, shown on the contract drawings and described by or referred to in the contract bills, in return for a promise by the building owner to pay for that work at the rate agreed. For the various types of contract you are recommended to refer to the books listed in the section 'Further Reading'. (It is not possible in this short guide to enter into a detailed analysis of the different contracts.)

Articles of Agreement

The actual contract between the building owner (usually the client) and the contractor. The formal parts are at the beginning of the contract forms.

Contract Bill

The fully priced bills of quantities that form part of the contract documents. Not all contracts have bills – a specification may be sufficient with small contracts.

Contract Drawings

The drawings, illustrating the scope of the contract, are agreed by all parties as representing the work as measured in the contract bills or as estimated by the contractor. The drawings on which the tender was based and submitted.

Bills of Quantities (the 'Bill')

Quantities of materials with descriptions on which an estimator fills in prices when preparing a tender. Bills of quantities are normally based on the various trades or elements, but can also be based on the sequence of building, when they are known as operational bills.

Specification (the 'Spec')
Describes precisely the materials and workmanship, the quality and the work to be done. Quantities are not usually given, as in the bills of quantities, although they can be. Materials to be used are described first, followed by the actual work to be done. Everything is included which, with the drawings, is necessary to define how the building is to be built. The production of the Specification is the responsibility of the architect.

Prime Cost Sum (PC sum)
A sum provided for work or services to be executed by a nominated subcontractor, a statutory authority or a public undertaking or for materials or goods to be obtained from a nominated supplier. Such sum shall be deemed to be exclusive of any profit required by the general contractor and provision shall be made for the addition thereof. (Definition in the *Standard Method of Measurement for Building Works*). Note that a Statutory Authority was generally an organisation legally authorised by public statute to provide a service for the general public – such as a Water, Gas or Electricity Board, but recent privatisation may have altered these legal responsibilities.

Provisional Sum (PS)
A sum provided for work or for costs that cannot be entirely foreseen, defined or detailed at the time the tendering documents are issued. (Definition in the *Standard Method of Measurement for Building Works*).

Liquidated and Ascertained Damages (LADs)
A sum of money specified in the contract to cover the expected cost to the client if the contractor commits a specified breach or fails to complete the contract within the specified time. For example, it could include the rent on an existing property if the new property is not available for occupation.

Contingency Sum
A provisional figure sometimes included to cover what is unknown at the time of tendering, such as an area of the building work where some unknown factor may occur with financial or programming consequences.

Schedule
A tabular or classified description or definition for specific performance, form, quality, quantity, purpose, etc., of value where a number of items of like kind is to be described and recorded.

Competitive Tender
An offer by one party to provide goods or services or undertake works for another party in return for a specified sum of money. 'Going out to tender' means sending out tender documents (bills of quantities, drawings, conditions, etc.) to a number of contractors or subcontractors in competition, with a stipulated time for returning their tenders, which are treated as confidential and opened altogether at a specific time.

Negotiated Tender
A single tender negotiated between two parties, preferably by building up a

price or prices in direct relation to an agreed basis or document.

Contractor

A firm of builders which, as a party to a building contract, is responsible for the organisation, management and execution of the whole of the work comprised in that contract. Sometimes referred to as the general or main contractor to differentiate the firm from subcontractors. In the contractor's organisation you may encounter the following personnel:

(a) Contracts manager and/or project manager – responsible for looking after a number of projects and contracts, and who operates from the contracting firm's office and not the site.

(b) General foreman – often called the site agent or site manager. There may also be trades foremen and sub-contractors will often have their own foremen.

(c) Contractor's surveyor – the contractor's own quantity surveyor, who will measure work and agree measurements, etc., with the client's quantity surveyor.

(d) Site engineer – part of the contractor's team as opposed to the client's engineer – responsible, for example, for setting out levels, etc.

(e) Various local expressions, such as 'brickie' for the bricklayer, 'chippy' for the joiner or 'sparks' for the electrician.

Nominated Subcontractor

A person nominated or named by the architect to execute work or to supply and fix materials or goods through the main contractor.

Nominated Supplier

A specialist, merchant, or tradesman nominated by the architect to supply materials or goods to the main contractor. Although there is no legal difference between a 'quotation' and an 'estimate', it is often colloquially assumed a quotation is a firm price, subject to specified conditions, such as being held for a certain length of time, while an estimate is only an approximate figure which cannot be treated with any certainty.

Architect's Instructions (AIs)

The issue of directions which the architect is empowered to make to the contractor under the conditions of a building contract, e.g. when amplification or changes are necessary, as building work proceeds, may include variations.

Variations

The alteration or modification of the design, quality or quantity of the works as shown in the contract drawings and described by or referred to in the contract bill, or specification or schedule of work.

Fluctuations

Those items and expenses for which a contractor, if the contract allows for it, may make a claim for extra cost if their costs are increased after the tender date and such increases were outside the contractor's general contemplation at that date. Such items may refer to labour, materials and taxes.

Measured Work

Work for which there is no parallel or other provision in the bills. It is then 'measured' in accordance with agreed national standard method of measurement.

Financial Certificates

The architect certifies from time to time (generally related to the quantity surveyor's valuations) that a certain amount of work has been done during the course of the contract (at 'interim' stages) so a proportion of the money due to the contractor can be paid. The Final Certificate is issued after the expiry of the defects liability period, and once the defects have been put right.

Practical Completion

The point at which the architect certifies the building as being complete in accordance with the contract. At this point the architect authorises the release of the first half of the retention fund.

Defects Liability Period

The period commencing after the issue of the Certificate of Practical Completion. Its duration is usually six months or as stated in the contract. It may require the contractor to come back on site and to correct any defects. A Certificate of Making Good Defects is issued when work is complete. (It is sometimes incorrectly called the maintenance period.)

Schedule of Defects

A list of defects, shrinkages and other faults that appear within the defects liability period and which (depending on the contract) it is the contractor's responsibility to make good.

The majority of certificates, architect's instructions, etc., suitable for use with JCT contracts, are published as standard forms available from RIBA Publications, Construction House, 56-64 Leonard Street, London, EC2A 4LT and RIBA Bookshops.

6

Keeping in Touch

Practical Training

It is essential that you regularly fill in your Professional Experience and Development Record and get it signed by your Office Supervisor and by your Practical Training Adviser in your school at the recommended intervals.

Re-read the introductory chapters from time to time to remind yourself of the overall objectives of the scheme and to check that you are getting a reasonable range of experience.

If you think you are not getting a wide variety of experience discuss the position first of all with your boss. It is also sensible to keep your own day-to-day diary, where you can note down not only your main office activities, but also points of interest, reminders, names and addresses of people you meet, and when you met them. This form of record will be useful later when you want to refer to something or someone you met in your year in the office.

Also try to obtain copies of some of the better drawings and reports you may have done in the year, as part of your record of the things you have done. These can go in your portfolio and might be useful when you apply for your next job, but make sure the office is happy for you to do this. (You will need to do this in your second period of practical training in order to write your

report or case study as required for the Examination in Professional Practice.)

Try to keep in touch with others in the profession, by continuing to take or read the regular architectural and building journals, by making contact with the local RIBA society of architects and attending their talks and meetings (at the branch in the area where you are working and with events at RIBA HQ if you are in central London). There is much local goodwill and advice available and the local society is a useful means of keeping in touch and making friends in what may be initially a strange town.

Keep in touch with your school. Although the break from school may seem a welcome relief, you should nevertheless keep in touch. Schools arrange seminars or other events for students (and their bosses) from time to time. These are useful for comparing notes and seeing how your friends are getting on, as well as for stimulating discussion about office practice from the student's point of view. Make sure the school has your latest office and home addresses etc. In addition, many schools set work that must be submitted by specified deadlines – remember, work carried out in your 'year out' is part of the course.

It is valuable for your Practical Training

Adviser to receive feedback on both the
good and bad points you may have
experienced in the office and this will
also build up a picture of offices that
can help those coming after you. It also
helps identify any shortcomings in the
educational course you have received
so far. You may also need to keep your
local authority informed of your
position and whereabouts since this
may affect your application for a grant
for the following year. In some offices,
particularly local government ones, it is
normal practice for a report to be
prepared on everyone who is on a
probation period for the first six months,
even though you will only be there for a
year. You are entitled to see this report.
Ask if it is permissible for a copy to be
sent to your Practical Training Adviser.

7

Undertaking Private Work

Students are sometimes approached to undertake private architectural work. It can be seen as a useful way of supplementing funds. It might also seem an attractive opportunity to gain personal experience.

The RIBA strongly urges students to take serious note of the following before accepting any such invitations:

- Remember you are embarking on a legally binding commitment. Do not do so on a casual or informal basis. Seek proper advice (from your Practical Training Adviser, for example, or from an experienced architect).

- Do not allow people to form a mistaken opinion that you are an architect. (This might place you in contravention of the Architects Registration Act or Trades Description Act.)

- Never take on work that is beyond your capabilities or resources. In the eyes of the law, the standard of skill and care expected of you might still be that of an architect. A reduced fee, or even no fee at all, will not lessen your liability.

- Be extremely wary about giving advice on any property, either from a point of view of condition or potential. This survey area is one which even very experienced architects treat with caution, and is often excluded from their indemnity insurance cover.

- Remember that practising architecture is a risky business. Architects adopt sound practice principles in order to avoid or reduce the risk and cover the risk by adequate professional indemnity insurance.

8

Glossary

Architect
A person who is on the register of ARB.

Architectural assistant
An assistant without professional qualifications. The correct designation for a student.

Job architect
The architect directly responsible, under a principal or a more senior architect, for the overall conduct and control of a particular commission or project.

Principal architect
In private practice: one who carries legal and financial responsibility; in a public office: an architect with the title chief architect or its equivalent. Note that in local government a principal officer can be a senior job architect – the title 'Principal' is related to the staff grading system and not to professional status.

Chartered architect
A corporate member of the RIBA.

Architects Registration Board of the United Kingdom (ARB)
Under the Architects (Registration) Acts, 1931 to 1996, every person who calls himself an architect, or who carries on a business under any name, style or title containing the word 'architect', must be registered. Students are warned that any practice that uses the term 'architectural' advisers, designers or

consultants, may not contain a registered architect.

RIBA
Royal Institute of British Architects. The professional institute to which all qualified and registered architects may belong. There are considerable benefits in being a member and the majority of architects do belong to the RIBA, but it is not mandatory. Students are encouraged to join as student members and there are many benefits in doing so.

RIAS
Royal Incorporation of Architects in Scotland. The Scottish Architectural Institute, membership of which is open to all architects living and working in Scotland.

RSUA
Royal Society of Ulster Architects. The Northern Ireland Architectural Institute, membership of which is open to architects living or working in Northern Ireland.

RICS
Royal Institution of Chartered Surveyors – of which the QS is likely to be a member.

SfB system
A method of classification devised in Sweden for all aspects of building and related fields. It uses a series of

alphabetical and numerical symbols: for example, 'Fg' denotes bricks or blocks of clay and (21) denotes walls. These can be combined in two ways: (21)Fg means walls of brick or clay, and Fg(21) means bricks of clay in walls.

CI/SfB

Construction Industry SfB. Note that most manufacturers' trade literature now has a CI/SfB code on it, although your office may not use the system. The SfB/UDC system (UDC = Universal Decimal Classification) is an internationally standardised system of classification for all knowledge, and is combined with the SfB system where applicable to give more detailed sub-division and for fringe subjects not adequately covered. UNICLASS (Unified Classification for the Construction Industry) came on stream in 1997 and is intended to supersede CI/SfB. It includes all the topics covered by CI/SfB and CAWS (Common Arrangement of Work Sections for building works), and, in addition, presents some new tables and parts of tables, and a new project lifecycle classification.

CPI

Co-ordinated Project Information. CPI procedures are used to integrate architectural and engineering drawings, specifications and bills of quantities.

9

Further Reading

It is not suggested that you need to buy all these during your Year Out, but you will probably need to refer to them from time to time. Most of them should be in your office library.

Job hunting
Directories published by RIBA Publications:
RIBA Members.
RIBA Directory of Practices.
RIBA International Architects.
RIAS Directory of Scottish Chartered Architects Offices.

RSUA Year Book and Directory.

Directory of Official Architecture and Planning
(now incorporates Housing and Planning Year Book). Pitman, 1997.

Illustrated Directory of Architects.
Association of Consultant Architects.

Richardson, Melanie.
RIBA Guides for Part 1 students wishing to work in Europe.

Professional practice
Co-ordinated Project Information (CPI), Co-ordinated Project Information for Building Works, a guide with examples.

Greenstreet, R and Chappell D
Legal and Contractual Procedures for Architects.
Butterworth, 4th revised edition 1994.

Hill, M.
Small Practices: A Guide to Drawn Information.
RIBA Publications, 1999.

Luder, O.
Small Practices: A Guide to Keeping Out of Trouble.
RIBA Publications, 1999.

Martin, I.
Small Practices: A Guide to Marketing on a Shoestring.
RIBA Publications, 1999.

Parkyn, N.
Small Practices: A Guide to Graphic Presentations.
RIBA Publications, 1999.

RIBA Architect's Handbook of Practice Management.
RIBA Publications, 6th edition 1998.

Sharp, D.
The Business of Architectural Practice.
Collins, BSP Professional, 2nd revised edition 1991.

Starting a Practice.
RIBA Publications, 1999.

Willis, A. and George, W.N.B.
(revised Chappell and Willis)
The Architect in Practice.
Blackwell, 7th edition 1994.

Running the job
Architect's Job Book.
RIBA Publications, 6th edition 1996.

Green, R.
The Architect's Guide to Running a Job.
Butterworth, 5th revised edition 1995.

CDM Regulations
*Architect's Guide to Job Administration
under the CDM Regulations 1994.*
RIBA Publications, 1996.

*Managing Construction for Health
& Safety:*
Construction (Design and Management)
Regulations 1994: Approved Code of
Practice. 1995.

Letter writing
Chappell, D.
*Standard letters in
Architectural Practice.*
Blackwell, 2nd revised edition 1994.

Report writing
Chappell, D.
Report Writing for Architects.
Blackwell Science, 3rd edition 1996.

Specification writing
Willis, A.J. and C.J.
*Specification Writing for Architects and
Surveyors.*
Blackwell Science, 10th edition 1991.

Contract
Chappell, D.
*Understanding JCT Standard
Building Contracts.*
Spon, 4th edition 1995.

Chappell, D.
*Contractual Correspondence
for Architects.*
Blackwell Science, 3rd edition 1996.

Cox, S. and Clamp, H.
Which Contract?
RIBA Publications, 2nd edition 1999.

Greenstreet, B. and Chappell, D.
*Legal and Contractual Procedures
for Architects.*
Butterworth, 4th edition 1994.

Lupton, S.
Guide to JCT98.
RIBA Publications, 1999.

Lupton, S.
Guide to IFC98.
RIBA Publications, 2000.

Lupton, S.
Guide to MW98.
RIBA Publications, 1999.

Powell-Smith, V. and Chappell, D.
Building Contract Dictionary.
Legal Studies and Services, 2nd revised
edition 1990.

Building regulations
Anstey, J.
Party Walls and what to do with them.
RICS Books, 4th edition 1996.

Architect's Guide to Job Administration: The Party Wall etc. Act 1996.
RIBA Publications, 1997.

Whyte, W.S., Powell-Smith V. and Billington, M.J.
Building Regulations.
BSP, 1995.

Planning
Cullingworth, J.B.
Town and Country Planning in Britain.
Allen & Unwin, 11th edition 1994.

Telling, A.E. and Duxbury R.M.C.
Planning Law & Procedure.
Butterworth, 10th edition 1994.

Dictionaries and reference
Haverstock, H.
The Building Design Easibrief.
Morgan Grampian, 1993.

Brett, P.
An Illustrated Dictionary of Building.
Butterworth-Heinemann, 2nd edition 1997.

Penton, J.
The Disability Discrimination Act: Inclusion – a workbook for building owners, facilities managers and architects.
RIBA Publications, 1999.

Scott, J. S. and Maclean J.H.
Penguin Dictionary of Building.
Penguin Books, 4th revised edition 1993.

Architects' Legal Handbook.
Butterworth, 6th edition 1996.

New Metric Handbook.
Butterworth-Heinemann, 1996.

Various trade and product manuals
The following is only a very brief selection:

Architects Standard Catalogue.
Barbour Compendium of Building Products.
Brick Development Assn. Design Note 3: Brickwork Dimension Tables.
Hepworth Drainage Manual.
Redland Roofing Manual.
RIBA Product Selector.

the *Baby Boomers* (General Board of Discipleship, 1989); workbook pages 30–33 and video.

19 See *Kicking Habits: Welcome Relief for Addicted Churches*, by Thomas G. Bandy (Abingdon Press, 1997); pages 89-96.

20 Adapted from "Which Fall Campaign?" by Donald W. Joiner, in *Celebrate Stewardship, Vol. 11, No. 1* (General Board of Discipleship of The United Methodist Church). Used by permission.

21 Discussed in *Right on the Money: Messages for Spiritual Growth Through Giving*, by Brian Bauknight (Discipleship Resources, 1993).

22 See *Preaching for Giving: Proclaiming Financial Stewardship With Holy Boldness*, by Timothy J. Bagwell (Discipleship Resources, 1993); page 49.

23 See "The liturgy of abundance, the myth of scarcity," by Walter Brueggemann, in *The Christian Century*, March 24-31, 1999; pages 342-347.

24 See *Stewardship of Lifestyle: A Resource for Helping Persons and Churches Develop a Lifestyle That Expresses Christian Stewardship*, by Paul M. Dietterich (The Center for Parish Development, 1986); page 54-71.

25 From *Aurora Leigh*, "Seventh Book," by Elizabeth Barrett Browning, 1864.